The Ohio State University Press/*The Journal* Award in Poetry

men as trees walking

poems by
Kevin Honold

THE OHIO STATE UNIVERSITY PRESS • COLUMBUS

Library of Congress Cataloging-in-Publication Data
Honold, Kevin, 1969–
  Men as trees walking / Kevin Honold.
      p. cm. — (The Ohio State University Press/The journal award in poetry)
  Includes bibliographical references.
  ISBN-13: 978-0-8142-5176-8 (pbk. : alk. paper)
  ISBN-10: 0-8142-5176-5 (pbk. : alk. paper)
  ISBN-13: 978-0-8142-9242-6 (cd-rom)
  1. American poetry—21st century. I. Title. II. Series: Ohio State University Press/The journal
award in poetry.
  PS3608.O4946M46 2010
  811'.6—dc22
                                    2010011155
This book is available in the following editions:

Paper (ISBN 978-0-89142-5176-8)
CD-ROM (ISBN 978-0-8142-9242-6)

Cover design by Fulcrum Creatives.
Type set in ITC Stone Serif.
Text design and typesetting by Jennifer Shoffey Forsythe.
Printed by Bookmobile.

♾ The paper used in this publication meets the minimum requirements of the American National
Standard for Information Sciences—Permanence of Paper for Printed Library Materials. ANSI
Z39.48-1992.

9 8 7 6 5 4 3 2 1

And he cam to bethsayda, and they brought a blynde man unto him and desyred hym, to touche him. And he caught the blinde by the honde, and ledd hym out off the toune, and spat in hys eyes and put hys hondes apon hym, and axed him yf he sawe enythinge, and he loked up and sayde: I se men, For I se them walke as they were trees.

Tyndale's Newe Testament, 1526

Contents

part iv

Stalingrad

We could learn things from each other.
I could tell you how it felt to hit that buck,
doing sixty-five in a loaded panel truck,
how it skidded forty feet on its back, hooves
kicking at the bright winter air,
antler tines scratching pea gravel from the asphalt.

You could tell me why it stood again, and walked.

You could tell me where the broken animals
go to die or worse, some dark bestiary
by the roadside, a camouflaged field station tended
lovingly by the homeless who shuffle barefoot
from bed to bed in butcher aprons
sewn with big red crosses.

I'll pour us some drinks.

On a night like this, Paulus' Sixth Army
was cut off in the burning city, caught
on the wrong side of the Don by a classic
pincer maneuver lifted straight from the Nazis' own book.
When the frost line measured a half meter they
began to eat the mules and the draft horses.

Read this book in the snow, the soldier wrote,

that you might know what cold is. Manstein's men
were cut to pieces trying to break in with supplies but
*Was this not the greatest love? To give your life
for a friend?* What do I know?
I know a lost cause when I read one. I know that those
grenadiers crouched on the tanks' backs are ghosts by now.

Skeletons in coal bucket helmets.

Twelve years later a few came back, arriving
uninvited at the platform in Berlin, paroled
from the timbercamp archipelago. 1955. Elvis
and the *Wirtschaftswunder.* Fieldgray stickmen waiting
futilely for remarried wives, muttering in Russian,
embarrassments to the busy new Republic.

The rest are still out there,

moving under cover of darkness, moving north
and west toward friendly lines,
fretting over forgotten passwords.
How will they answer the sentry's challenge?
What password can they offer? Argonaut? Obelisk?
Galileo? *Verdammt,* we could guess all night.

part i

Morning Issue

The moon rises from a hedge of cloud,
smooth as an ibis' head and trembling
with bad news for pharaoh. Deliverymen
shoulder bundles of papers out to their dark trucks and

return emptyhanded to the warehouse light trailing
blank speech banners of breath.
When the trucks are loaded the men
stand on the sidewalk and smoke, bootdeep in a yellow

scree of streetlight. I stand beneath a tree and watch them
and listen to my blood run, guessing at the news and jealous
of anyone with heavy lifting to do, or piecework
to keep the hands busy, as dawn

raises a bruised shoulder over the rooftops,
buckled and speechless from her long night of digging.

At the Central Missouri Produce Auction

Black plastic flats of lipstick-colored impatiens, a pansy
planted in a leftfooted workboot. The auctioneer
on the platform is flanked by a boatjawed
scribe sporting a noon shadow
and he sings the price of flowers in a voice part

banjo breakdown. Wild grasses bear
clusters of tiny flowers like
lesser constellations. Three Mennonites stand
at the foot of the platform in open-necked shirts wearing
the tough whiskers and straw

fedoras of Rumanian gangsters. Cyclamen
shaped like propeller screws
O I love the Spring says the old woman in a High Dutch
bonnet behind me. Off in the corner lurk
a pair of newlyweds wearing that hunted look

among the racks of painted daisies,
the gumdrops made gaudy with petals. I carry a flat of pansies
into the rain, past a row of blinkered
horses hitched to a post, a muddy lot filled
with bicycles and wagons and wooden-wheeled tractors.

And over beside the state route, beneath
a great dripping tree, a girl in a white dress
holds an infant in her lap, woman and child like
an ideogram for loneliness, a thought picture of
scattered showers from Kansas City to Shawnee Town.

Spaceman

I wrote letters to the former astronaut
who lived alone on an Ohio farm.
I asked him what the world looked like
from far away. Was the sun

bright and warm like we feel it or glossy
and cool like a coin? Were the stars closer?
Could you hear anything?
Were you scared? But he never wrote back.

From the empty mailbox
I walked into the woods and wondered
what I'd say if I met him, then and there,
standing beneath the branches. The whirr

of his respirator, the tap of valves
opening, shutting, drawing
Ohio's cool October air as he
stood before me and breathed

with the patience of a safecracker.
What did it feel like to look back? To be gone?
My face reflected in the visor's dark shine.
Patches of flags on his shoulders.

Overlook Park

A waste gas flame pelts the air. The engines at the railhead
back and shunt and haul chains of coal cars and gas
hoppers as they have all day. The braking of steel wheels fills the air,

god's damp finger tracing the rim of a desert, the unholy
music of the spheres to which swallows flit and veer, hunting
    midges.
The sun sinks and all that's left is a plume of candyapple light

rising to the one long breath of evening traffic, the heartbeat
of tractor trailers gearing up and down, and the first star appears
with her hair uncombed and not a word about where she's been.

The Anglo-Afghan Wars

February in the pool hall, the girls are pale
and their laughter is dry as dead leaves.
The men circle the tables with sticks and eye the green
or wait with cues planted between their feet
like those Swiss sentries posted with halberds at the Vatican.

We play for beers, scrutinize the table like a
map of the world's spread on it, like we're all members
of the imperial staff scooting color-coded flags with shuffle cues.
Bishop white and dragoon green. Red for edict. Blue for warhorse.
When I called the six in the corner she said

your Sikh-officered sepoys are quite reliable, true, but those
dismounted Yorkshires are no match for my Pathan cavalry and she
was right. To this day, the odd English bone will be turned
by a plow blade in the poppy fields, drawn to the surface
by the heat of the sun, or, maybe, the tread of the plowman's feet.

Walking out of there one afternoon, I fell and hit my head on the
    ice.
There followed this slow coming-to, a slow walk home, my arms
and legs swinging lightly as if worked with sticks and string, and
    everything
appeared innocent and new like a crayon drawing on powder blue
construction paper. Big combers of wind topped with spindrift

curlicues, green eyelash strokes of birds on the wing, canted
pillars of lemon sun. Two people
on the sidewalk smiling and holding hands
beneath seven raspberry clouds.

Storm Clouds

Flotilla of decommissioned colliers, dredged up and
patched with scrap. Last week, they marauded over horse latitude
waters and left two tankers bleeding. They come on for an hour and
    loom

slatternly, vitrified, saltcrusted. Irish cliffs gone walking.
Lightning splits the sky and blows the neighborhood transformer,
casts the little houses into dusk. The unhappy

husbands stare at the rain through window panes
that creak like mice inside their frames and the wives
open books and read, the anger dying inside them. It's very strange.

After the storm, the clouds drop guy wires and dock,
pearl dirigibles shadowing the houses, determined
to defend us from the heat of the sun,
flushing to crimson with the evening.

Fire Department Exercise

They burn the abandoned house down
room by room. They file in and out with axes, trailing smoke
from the hems of their coats, shouting through respirators.
They stand on the lawn to watch torsos of flame

leap from upper windows, then file in again.
The veterans lounge at the ladder truck and loose
vicious hawsers of water from the hose,
cutting in half those errant flames that lean too far over the sills.

By evening only a doorframe and a chimney stand
in a filigree of embers, and the neighbors on the sidewalk
fold their lawnchairs and call their children home.
The doorjamb bears some spraypainted symbol,

inscrutable in rescue red, blood harbinger of the visitant angel,
and the little girl perched on her father's
hip clutches a cola can and gravely
whispers into his ear.

Achaeans

Real crackerjacks, they were. I woke up before work
just to read how they died, how the homesick sons of Hellas
aimed the ships' eyes, painted red on the prows and
livid with froth, away from the shore where the companions lay,

where a forest of planted oars marks the graves.
When I crossed the Ohio in a pipe truck that morning
the hulls I saw spin down the green water,
helpless before a quartering wind, breaking apart

on the pylons of the Covington bridge.
I saw the survivors paddling broken oars to shore.
Potholes banged the copper pipe in the racks behind me
like the clangor of speared Achaeans rattling

in their armor as they hit the sand, cut down
by the hundred in windrows like wheat by sickles.
Homer used up all the killing similes but I got
an acetylene tank with a Turbo-Torch

and fifteen foot of hose. I can sweat copper. Fix leaks.

Journeyman

i.

His liquor breath mixes with the cold chemical
scents of solder paste and pipe dope
as we idle on the bridge packed
with stalled traffic from Newport
to Cincinnati. Below the bridge barrier, a coal barge
butts a comber of froth with its blunt prow.
She's jealous about this woman that moved in
down the street, he says. Can you believe that?
Short bald bignose fucker like me.
Smiling in disbelief, boots kicked up on the muddy dash,
watching the riverwater bend in long rills
around the pylons of the L & N trestle.
God I'm lucky.

ii.

We climb to the last floor where
he opens a window and taps a finger
to his shut mouth, quiet, and I bend out to look.
        From a nest wedged
into a joint in the sandstone the hawk cocks an eye

a wing's length from her shoulder.
Fledgling feathers shiver among her chicks' fluff
and their gray down blazes in the windshear.
He taps my back, *don't scare em,*
and I shut the window. *Don't tell anyone.*

He pulls two beer bottles from a fusebox
and talks about England and hawking and I picture
men in green hunting frocks
at the edge of a deep wood, golden birds

rising from their wrists, straining
at the jesses and never quite there.

iii.

Thursday evenings in an industrial park warehouse
we study the Code as related by a Southwest
Ohio Master Plumbers' Association
instructor, vent stacks and angle-of-slope,
gravity tanks and tie-ins, pressure tests, how many
offsets are allowed

between the vertical and the road.
On break we stand in the snow beside
a pipe truck, drink beer and smoke cigarettes.
Quiz at quarter-to-nine, blue shirts in a circle
in fluorescent light. It's all bullshit,
someone says, but most of us think hard over the questions

with an eye to the faroff day when we
earn our journeyman's cards, make real money,
walk onto jobsites with an easy slang for tools,
wiser than any book method, peers
to the journeymen who trained us because
then we'd be licensed, too, in a trade
you could be proud to hate.

Cincinnati

Dead leaves pressed palmdown on the plastic
roof of the bus shelter, wet concrete seeded
with cigarette butts and gum, the pedestrians' shoes
that hardly touch the ground. That night their faces

return to me like voices over a river, so translucent
I can't believe them, and even
my books try to trick me. Thoreau teasing those
almshouse halfwits who happened by his cabin, how

he couldn't seem to puzzle the mind
of that French Canadian woodcutter who sang
through the trees with his axe on his shoulder, who
shot his pistol at the sky for no good reason at all

and bolted chunks of fried woodchuck
with gulps of coffee, pissed the letters of his
hometown in the snow.
What's so hard to understand, Henry?

Crossing the Mississippi River

When the storm passes, the sky
breaks open its enginery of stars.
I guess there's something symbolic in crossing this river

but whatever it meant to pioneers is lost to me.
I don't know what De Soto said or what
his starving soldiers were thinking when they arrived

at the banks of this river, far to the south in Arkansas.
Shivering in pigskin, speechless in the mud, watching giant trees
pass facedown in the flood,

borne senselessly to an unknown sea.
They might have tossed coins in the water,
turned one by one away to hunt

berries in the forest. The wind in the leaves
above their helmets burrs like truck tires
on bridge decking, and only

the bloodhounds holding their ground,
dipping their old heads to the water for a drink.

part ii

The Velvet Revolution, 1989–1990

There was hope back then. In the motor pool with
an early discharge application in my pocket,
I listened to good news on Armed Forces Radio. Everywhere,
armies were disbanding. In the high latitudes, a man
stepped out of a cell on Robben Island, shook the guards' hands,
   took

the ferry home and ran for office. In Dresden a soldier
threw a grappling hook over Stalin's iron shoulder and handed
the rope's end to some idle kids. Policemen
holstered their truncheons and granted safe passage
to candlelight vigils in Leipziger Square that rivaled Nuremberg's

torchlight parades from the days before
it was flattened by night bombers. Rumor spread of a Soviet ruse
as we drove to the border where we met columns
of westbound East Germans and found
a worker's family smiling beside a brokendown Trabi whose

two-stroke engine had died of a thrown cylinder,
just this side of the fence. We traded Marlboros for chocolate cake
and aluminum pfennigs stamped with the hammer-and-sickle,
smiled for pictures, as the Guards Armies drove back to Russia
with ten billion in Deutsche Marks and a parting assurance to Bonn

that they would buy decent housing (and some food
um Gottes willen!) for the officers' kids and the soldiers' wives.
What did I care how they spent it? I was waiting for a plane ride
back to the world, to start my real life with GI Bill money
and unspent leave pay. Then I saw a white squirrel

on the barracks' commons and the Slovenes
started digging weapons pits and the Club of Rome
gave mother earth fifty years to live and I
found you sitting heartbroken on the bunk because

all the early releases had been cancelled, all enlistments

indefinitely and peremptorily extended.
There wasn't much to say. Six months later we sat
crosslegged on a dune at night and watched the oil well fires,
the livid suture of the skyline. My heart felt wattled together
from pig hair and mud and straw and I couldn't

bring myself to tell you how fucking beautiful it was.

i. Nuremberg, 1990

We bought hash off the Turks and cocaine
and walked the snowcovered cobblestone lanes
to the lowlit places that never closed.
I drank until I couldn't feel drunk
anymore though its warmth made strangers

kinder and we ended up in the alleys
where women shivered, leaning
their pale faces from the windows.
Their hair smoldered with the rooms' blue light
as they dropped friendly questions to the GIs

on the street. Hey, soldat, is it cold to you?
On the U-bahn back to the barracks the few scattered
riders slouched at the windows
counting station lights and we deboarded at Riyadh
International and stood on the puddled tarmac breathing

jet fuel fumes, humidity, palms. My friend
watched a fighter-bomber taxi, lift, and bank away
and its blazing tail was a little gold jag buried
in the damp of each eye.

ii. Sortie

We sat in the sand beyond
the perimeter ditch and kept
long intervals of silence between us,
the scarlet and brickdust-colored clouds

at sunset like rain sheeting down a window.
The bombers' sweptback wings glinted
with the last light,
like signal mirrors.

They banked in a lazy wheel across
nations of sky, then returned
as if they'd forgotten something.
I imagine holding in my hands

a tiny instrument, like the ones
that guide the bombers home. The thin
black needle shivering on the dial. The unlikely
weight of the lodestone in my palm.

iii. Men as Trees Walking

A truck storms out of the desert hauling
cases of bottled water and a laundry sack full of letters. A sergeant
stands in the truckbed and calls names.

Atencio Hobart McGrath Lee

We listen in green camouflage,
disguised for an unlikely season, for a land of trees
and treeshadow. The called ones smile like they've been found.

Palmerton Pfeifer Womack Salinas

When the last name is read,
the unlucky walk off in any direction, fatigues of mottled foliage
drifting into the desert, hands in pockets,

searching for quiet spots to root. Somwhere are cars
parked on a steep hill, a collection of out-of-state
beer cans, a buffalo nickel.

Thirteen dollars I once found sweeping out
a bar. A hideout I built in the woods
with scrap pressboard and eight-penny nails.

iv. Across the Border

Flights of rockets arc the sky, balling
through the sound barrier and tracing grand trajectories.
Engineers touch off explosives, blast an esplanade

through the house-high berm. They rise in a fallout of sand
and huddle to discuss the hole they've made.
We tear off name and regimental patches, pocket crucifixes

and medallions of saints Anthony or Christopher.
As we idle in column I picture a landscape
scarred with trench lines and antitank ditches and wonder

who's waiting on the far side of the sand wall, an army hunched
beneath a fall of rockets, angry men gripping rifles
in countless rifle pits. Tanks buried turret-deep in the sand,

barrels raised to test the wind. Kilometers of concertina wire.
But when we roll in single file through the gap we find a similar des-
    ert,
the same stillness we left behind, nothing for several miles. And then

a lone Iraqi soldier standing to the side of the column with his
hands clasped together. Unshaven,
without a helmet. Pleading for his life, or a ride.

V.

The M1s' wide tracks kick up breakers
of sand like tractor trailers barreling down
a flooded turnpike. A row of T-62s
and BMPs mills on a ridge, rolling
into position or turning away,

very short on time to find the range.
The M1s' main guns fire,
knocking at the sky and the incandescent rounds
travel so slowly across the sand
you can follow with your eyes as the shot

trails away to its target. Smoke columns
tilt before the breeze. We pass their half-buried armor, and a tank
whose turret lies upsidedown beside it
like a hat blown off in a sudden wind. Fighter bombers
dive out of the clouds and the air shudders with Gatling gunbursts,

antitank cannonfire. Bareheaded
enemy crewmen run without weapons
across the desert, toward the far side of the horizon.
Helicopters beat through the smoke, casting
no shadows as they race above the ground.

vi. Rearguard Action

A low ceiling of ash from the burning wells buries
the stars. Scattered hulls of vehicles burn and black
smoke chuffs from turret hatches. An APC
rumbles in a jar of gold light, a fiery semblance of itself,

broken and pieced back together with flames. In the morning
the Iraqi troop carrier rolls toward us on its broken wheel,
steel lambent with rain, the sun a chinese
lantern behind the smoke. The M1 takes aim

like a proper authority over a broken horse.
A bright round strings the desert, the carrier
rocks once in place and burns, and no one climbs out.
The round is a white trace across the windshield.
A helicopter rockets the flames.

vii.

The helicopters approach low to the ground and their blades
buffet the air. They hover head-high,
specters on the desert, just visible
through seventy meters of darkness if

you look left-of-center, blink, and hold your breath.
Pilots' fingers hardwired to rocket tubes,
heat sensitive as moths, registering the lime phosphorescence
of our bodies through nightvision, our chemical suits

as green as any enemy's jacket.
The sergeant shouts into the handset *identify friendlies*
on the ground, friendly forces to your southwest but
there's no response and we step away from the vehicles

and wave our arms for recognition
at the pilots who are holding fire, trying to figure us out.

viii. Convoy

As we pass through a town near Nasiriyah small boys
spill from doorways, drawn from sunless
rooms by the novelty of traffic.
They rush the column and line the track, exhaust and dust,
big shy smiles for any army,

for big guns on parade.
They hop a pantomime of gunplay and wave, loose
shouts of hunger and greeting. Pulled back
by their mothers from the roadside, shaken, scolded
with harsh lectures, they vanish

in the folds of black robes. An old man in a suit coat,
his head wrapped in red cloth, stands at the end
of a deserted lane, singular as a post.
Lone women wave their gloved hands and plead
for food or redress, name us behind their veils.

Ration packets are tossed from windows and turret
hatches, and some packets
are slung with a will and find marks.
A woman's leg, a boy's chest. The boys gather the packets up
with puzzled smiles. Helicopters buzz the town,

tailbooms lifted high, the air throttled in the low sweep.

ix. Ceasefire with Smoke and Sunspots

The sun dim as a pocketwatch lid through the carbon,
flawed with three dark spots
like dints from a finish hammer.

Vehicles burn. The wind wrestles the pillars of black
smoke to the ground. Enemy soldiers
walk from a field of burning armor

with their hands on their heads or arms spread wide
to signify emptiness. They grimace at the cigarettes
and ration packets we give them, teeth bared

in a chronic flinch. Their faces set in a dull ache
as they sit crosslegged in the sand, concussed to silence,
lolling, wired. Early afternoon,

we stand in blowing sand, bandannas tied
banditwise around our faces. In the green shadow
of the oil smoke we try to make out the president's speech

on the shortwave but the wind takes most of the words away.
Maybe there was a panic about the spots on the sun and
he was speaking to the nation's fears, relating

the science as he knew it, reiterating the constancy of the stars,
so we drive further over a plain crosshatched
by hundreds of treads, past the burning armor, past
the crewman sprawled facedown in the sand.

part iii

The Groves of Ba'al

Remember the weird stories in scripture?
  Yeah. The sea monsters even,
  even they nursed their young.
And the evil daughters,
become cruel as ostriches in the wilderness?
  Yeah. I was an ostrich.

In the foothills east of Chillicothe,
  beneath the golden maples,
  in the deer bed tamped in tall grass,
remember how the moon rose
through the sycamore
  molting her horns in the branches

and we walked down South Main holding
  our faces in our hands?
Remember how they punished everyone
to spread the shame out evenly?
  they took the young men to heaven
  and made the children chop the wood

Spring

Between the cornrows, henbit sprouts
in lilac patches on the mould. Blue
frost in the furrow shadow. A redtail

kites in the cool wind, April, time
to rededicate ourselves to beautiful things. In the mind's eye,
an iridescent pinwheel spins above

the newly tilled tomato garden and the trash along
the fence has been picked up.
Leave it for another time.

Last year's cornstalks are hacked to hard angles, line
on line of cuneiform script telling of an ancient king's
journey to the underworld where he comes upon

a garden turned to glass, stone fruit ripe with gemlight,
temple bells melted around their clappers
like moonflowers at daybreak fold

their stamens in their petals.
In the cool of the garden, the childless sit on the ground and sigh.
The unburied beg for water. And those

who went missing lean
crossarmed against the trees.

Downtown

The father pours seeds into his little girl's
palms and pigeons rise to perch
doubtfully on her fingertips, to feed.
She laughs holding handfuls

of wings as if complicit in some sorcery,
caught in an act of two purple fires.
She lifts her hands and the flames disperse and
the clouds begin to break after what

seems like days. The brand new quality of sunlight
on their faces. The sudden company of my shadow.

Box Truck Drivers

Because grace wears thin, you lie in bed
at 5 AM and craft headlines for a small article buried
in the Metro section—*Found in Snow among Glass and Splinters,*
or, *Man Crosses Median.* You hope god's otherwise

occupied, busy inciting a riot in Kinshasa with a street-
corner tirade against the Lexus class, haranguing
the mob through the smoke of tire fires. Busy rallying
Grozny's defenders amid the eminently

defensible rubble then conducting a brilliant
fighting-withdrawal to the Caucasus. Busy
painting Balkan crosses in black acrylic on his new
model-kit Stuka. What's he do all day, anyway?

Help the Great Hare pile dirt up for the drowning
Mound Builders? Sweep the horn-rimmed reading glasses
at Birkenau into drifts of buckled sparrow wings?
Storm at his aides-de-camp inside his bunker because, where he lives,

it's always the Summer of '44 and Army Group Center
is splintering before Zhukov's tanks? I can't say.
Creeping along with the backup on I-75, a foil sack of corn chips
pressed like a feedbag to my face, past the wreckage on the shoulder

where the uninjured stand close together with their
hands over their mouths because
the words they might speak belong to that hard dead language
we used to covenant with wolves in.

Sweet Mary what a mess.

Conquistadors

Deep woods of those days,
canopy shadow and windstorm ruin.
Spanish soldiers lived in there,
bivouacked among

the fallen trunks.
After mass Sunday mornings I found
the tepid ash of their abandoned fire.
I saw the corrosion on battered armor,

heard the low voices of exile,
many years' march
from the beaches of their burnt ships.
One morning I watched them lead

black horses on foot through the trees.
They carried rusted swords
on their shoulders and the wind
blew through the pines' crowns like a trumpet.

Winter Night at the Indianapolis Greyhound Station

Travelers slouch behind low barricades of baggage, backs
to the tiled walls. Two men paired in low conversation
lean at a column, smoothing worn bills with their fingers,

faces hidden in hoods like traders at a camel fair.
Children's faces sink into heavy coats as they fall asleep.
We observe one another like cities

on the same broad plain, scanning for relief columns,
vulnerable to the clouds, measuring the distances
through the glare as though from so many windows,

and the eyes we meet turn away to the firmament
of flaked blue paint, the ranked fluorescent suns.

After the Flood

On the frozen Wabash, ice floes broad as tabletops
twist slowly in the current and do blind
hurt to their kind as they spin. The air is filled

with the bright clash of the ice like glass
fed through a flour mill. A cardinal hops over
newly risen ground, over the black

leaves, questioning the falling sun. He sings, stormflag
red on the lip of the bank,
claiming a patch for his god.

The sun falls behind the smokestacks
and I rouse the old servant and walk back to the road,
between the mudbooted trees braced

with halyards of creeper. The flood has swept off
the undergrowth and carved roman roads
through the woods, highways studded

with pale stone and roots' knees, and I can't
decide if the sound in my ears
is the rasp of the milling floes or

the old servant chastising the trees
or if it's just me, talking to myself again,
salaamed by strange birds.

Bus Pass

He sits in the back of the bus with his hands
folded in his lap and looks through rainsqualid
windows at people in doorways. He wears a laminated
bus pass clipped to his breast pocket flap and smells like
bourbon and mentholyptus. Makes no mention

of the handcuffed man pressed bellydown on the
trunk of a cruiser, fingers splayed like a cock's brush
behind his back. When I speak to him, he winces as though my
voice were some painful sound that less resembles words
than the shudder in the waterline just before it bursts.

When the light changes and the bus moves he composes himself
sufficiently to comment sensibly on the ballgame.
The travesty of leaving thirteen runners stranded, the desperate
need for some middle relief, the driver's
eye watching him from a skewed and rattly mirror.

Birds in March

Past the noise of traffic and the in-and-out-
bound aircare helicopters, the robin in the grass
hears the worm turn in its sleep. The robins

ranged the city park all winter in mixed flocks of blackcapped
chickadees and chipping sparrows and
cardinals from tree to tree, ransacking the shadows,

singing. Gray leaves fell to the tolling
church bells that called and called to people who
wouldn't answer. Snowflakes from the porcelain sky like

magnetic interference from some dying star, a haze in the air
that carried voices. But today, the good spirits of the bells
ring over the city and I hurry down to the riverside

with my bird guide and my handbell to welcome Spring's
return, the purplecheeked ships parading in the breeze,
masts festooned with garlands of myrtle,

saffron streamers trailing like broken wings to the water.

Sparta

Four men in a Kroger parking lot lean
into a Bonneville, each to a window, and administer
a beating to the driver that makes the car

rock on its struts. Torsos swallowed by the tinted glass,
hightops planted batter-stance on the blacktop, shirts
untucked by the effort of cock-and-fire, cock-

and-fire, feet shuffling for a better angle.
A boy idles on his Huffy and watches from an empty
parking space as justice is meted in a neighborhood

cordoned by interstates and concrete jersey barriers
that hardly keep the crackheads in, or out.
Some day, when we're all seated quietly

on wooden chairs in a corridor awaiting our hearings
in the star chamber, the boy will be subpoenaed
to testify on behalf of six Canadian soldiers who

kicked to death every *Hitlerjugend* they found
as payback for killing Allied prisoners and
for dressing like trees. He idles and breathes the sweet

scent from the soap plants along the canal as July's heat
bathes him like a Spartan manchild was bathed,
with wine. Some day he, too, will join his brothers in battle,

shields lapped, advancing to tabors and pipes, and he'll wake
in the Spartan paradise, a young cedar beside a limpid stream
where his brothers are already cooling their feet,

their newly-healed bodies oiled and scented,
watching the girls toss bread to the ducks.

Orion the Hunter

The ghost in the machine never sleeps.
Prefers the attic, where he dons his rusty armor and swears
he's going to murder you. Kicks his dog.

Cries for no reason. Is constructing something
in the potato cellar that taxes the circuitry and sometimes, say,
when you're sitting on the porch, the ringing in your ears

will slacken and surge as the stars short out like fireflies.
If you fill your cell with gold and silver
he takes it all and declares the ransom insufficient and orders

the place filled to the ceiling again. Is legion,
and alone. Expert in the arts of woodland camouflage. Possessed
of courage of the uncommon 3 AM variety.

Will storm out of the house without warning,
leaving an unquietness that wakes you. Put your boots on.
Step outside. The moon has set, Venus will rise soon.

Orion stalks the far reaches of the sky
with his club and his dog. Relax.
Have a cigarette. He won't be back for hours.

Fourth of July

Listing on a lawn chair in the grass balancing
a gin tonic on the aluminum armrest, I feel
the fireworks thump like depth charges in my head
and imagine god pacing the bridge of His Majesty's Ship
Mooneshine, trolling the Channel waters for Nazi subs

while we smoke and sweat and stare through the turquoise
light of the gauges, twenty fathoms down and running low on air.
On this night of celebration we give thanks that the legions
of Gog and Magog remain a long way off, and it grows less
likely with each passing year that god will return to judge the cities,

not that anyone in this town would notice if he did. Love is truth,
Jesus said. Truth is love. After that, there wasn't much else to be
    done.
The redbaiting squirearchy of the suburbs sporting tribal tattoos
still fills the coliseum when the emperor arranges mortal
combats between maniacs. The tiger eats the faun

while the wildebeest look on. The Sun of Austerlitz is the same as
    that
which stood still for Joshua at Gibeon while his lord
dropped big rocks on the Amorites. Was the monster
that terrorized Antioch the same that shadowed Hannibal's army?
You know why they crucified that astronomer back then,

can you tell me again? What does it profiteth a man to gain
the whole world, and lose his soul? Isn't that fallacious?
I'm speaking up. I'm going to call the sun a redhot stone
and the moon a jar of clay and the soul a trapezoid, or a triangle.
Is calling the sun a stone still grounds for excommunication?

Anyway, I'll become famous, and my birthday
will be declared a holiday for schoolkids. But my greatest
achievement will be the knocking of the Pyramids down, those

despicable monuments to cruelty and pride.
How much cordite will I need to level them with the Nile?

How much will I need?

Tippecanoe State Park

The trees that winter starved stand over their dead branches like
ghosts over sloughed chains
and the birds of passage have come home

to reclaim their listening-posts by the water,
older by weeks of hard travel, disquieted
by the strange weathers and suns they've seen, the forests that never
   die.

Sunlight lies in long colors on the water, cedar and gold,
penny and green. A vulture
lights on a branch above us, wings spread wide to air. Machinelike,

it rakes the forest floor with its eyes, drops into a low glide
to strafe the creek rocks. I wish I could
identify every bird by song, or feather. I wish I could properly,

for once, describe in words a cardinal, in a manner
that didn't disappoint him.

part iv

Jupiter of the Wabash

The shell of an old car is sinking
inevitably into the ground. The sand is up
over the dash and rising. Maybe Pluto needs to borrow
a ride to get Persephone to the airstrip in time
for the annual visit with family.

Maybe it'll be decorated with wreaths of dead flowers and
entered into the harvest parade, scenes from the upper
world cut into the quarter-panels by demons with torches,
scorched crows and trees buffeted
by black flourishes of wind. When an eagle flew down

the middle of the river and I knew that
if it banked right, I would forthwith
embark on a bold adventure, triumph in many contests,
gain possession of rich estates and a castle where I carouse
until daybreak surrounded by damsels

craving boons, and I would acquire a sword whose
blade could wound the wind, in place of this old thing.
And if the bird banked left, the ground would open up and I'd
drop right into hell, but the bird kept
straight on so I went home to my

efficiency and ate macaroni and cheese and watched the news,
filled with the bonedeep sadness one
contracts in the presence of the gods. O doe-eyed
bride of the monarch of the realms of the dead,
I'm afraid I'll never find you.

"The Girl on the Bus Carried the Weight"

The girl on the bus carried the weight
of her child as one unused to a burden,
though happier for it. That night I lay awake and tended
the memory of her like a small fire to keep

bad spirits away. Love is a sleeping sickness, or a sad child
born once upon a time
to a thief and a cloud and left by a well

for the servants to find,
or the somnolent existence of whales
in subtropical seas, the diaphanous

puddle of sun overhead, the coda
and clang of kind strangers around you.

Three Ideas

i. US 62 east of El Paso

Wind turbines line the crest
of a ridge running along the highway,
bonewhite pinwheels, a clan
of cyclops bearing
the outlandish flowers of remorse.

ii. I-30 south of Little Rock

Thousands of migrating geese
in living lines ripple the sky, like
abbreviated ranks of combers in a blue bay
as viewed from a cliff or from a small
plane circling upsidedown.

iii. UP rail-line outside Willcox, Arizona

The shower passes. A heap of railroad
spikes gleams, speartips of meteoric iron
collected from an ancient battlefield.
The sky gazes frankly from every puddle.
Out on the desert, where the mountains
lose focus, where the absolute goes
to think itself, a blue cloud
furls a blue wing of rain.

Elpenor

Unwept, unburied, cast on the wide earth, I carried
a long stick into a field and spooked crows up
from the broken cornstalks.

That wasn't my intention at all. A hawk
skimmed over the transmission lines trimming its wings
and the trees faced out over the field,

biding in the steady drip of snowmelt from their crowns.
Evening fell with the scents of horses and wine
and starlight burned on the harrow teeth.

I heard the sound of a bowstring, the fleet
patter of wings, watched shadows moving at a crouch
through the trees and it was then I saw my old

companions running toward me and I
rejoiced at my salvation. I knew them
by the colors of the plumes on their helmets and wept

to see their careworn faces, their bloody armor,
and how in their weariness
they leaned on their spears for breath.

Borderlands

the 622 cardinal express from chicago to louisville has been delayed.
We apologize for any inconvenience

We'd give anything to understand why but Balaam's ass is
just bones that don't speak though you beat and beat and beat
them, and the gods are just statues trapped atop tall

pediments at Chicago's train station, sorry and naked, clutching
flagons of wine, holding their stone brows in their stone palms
as the public address intones another thirty minute

delay with no hint of remorse in its voice. A woman sits on the
    wooden bench
and folds articles of clothing, triple-knots the twine she uses
to secure her gear to her handcart, anything

until the transit cops turn her out to winter.
Old black men in the corner snuff butts
on the marble and plot insurrection over McDonald's cups

filled with Mogen David, heads bowed together like a
committee of correspondence from the days when Attucks
was a war cry, and one man lifts his head from the huddle to scan

the big hall for Tories. His eyes find mine and sack them.
The p.a. announces another delay. Christ.
There's a long train out in the countryside that may or may not ever
    arrive,

out in the tribal areas of Illinois-at-night, trolling
the hinterland, observed from hilltops by warriors wearing bird
    masks while
we slouch resigned on the benches and pull our jacket collars up and

measure the dumb minutes until we scuttle our boats and follow

a bad map into the jungle. Somewhere out there,
I have to believe, a railroad semaphore

will be seized will alarm bells, warning arms waving and
flashing its red furious eye, seven crows rising
from the littered cinders.

Ancient Greek Burial Customs

When I died they
bled and dried my body
and stuffed my chest with shreds of cloth
inscribed with throwaway lines
from a middling poet who died
unknown, unread. They sang a country

song and sealed me up in stone and
went away, my soul duly
restored to chaos.

Ages from now they'll
carry my body from the mountain
and drop me on a slab and probe
with latexed fingers the dusty
places where my heart once was.

They'll find instead words
in a dead language, some lines about
summer evenings, how he'll come for her at
the lighting of the lamps, singing that song,
and she'll meet him with a candle at the door.

The National Mall

national gallery of art

The wings of the angel who brings
Mary the good news are black as a scarlet tanager's, or white
as a snowy egret's, depending on the century.

A little more consistent is the postpartum
despair depicted on the Virgin's face through the ages,
and the winter birds with wings like claws. Here's Jerome

squatting improbably in rags in the desert before
a folio edition of his own Vulgate. There's
Jesus forever on his tree—never as he really was,

walking down some street
in sandals cut from Cooper tires, wagging
his bell in the air, decked in gunnysacks and a crown of blue stars.

Here's Adam being expelled from the garden
to a hard place in the shadow of the volcano where
the zigzag tracks of lava are like hairline seams

on a skull—well, I'm sorry to admit it, but
I've never seen a painting of Man's
Banishment I didn't like.

national zoo

The red crown crane perches
on one leg in the middleground
of her enclosure, sunk in a brown study, rapt

to hard truths. In the fairy bluebird's eyes
you can read the fate of the pygmy falcon, which

she'll meet beside some river. Scarlet

ibis, weaver bird, cedar of lebanon, don't
leave us here alone! Please, god,
send good dreams. Pastures and timber

to wander through, hand in hand with my soul.
Send buzzards tumbling in cloudshadow like
longforgotten names. Tell me

precisely the right things to say.

national museum of american history

It's a muggy day. The air blank and
thick as marshlight on the Mall. A transient
deadmarches over the blasted lawn reciting

his lines one last time. Strife is storms,
clouds, winds, separation. Love is a bringing-
together, a poor old couple in a mountain hovel who,
lucky day, show a kindness

to a pair of gods disguised in laborers' gear. To forgive
without fear, like the good bishop said. To love
one another. To accept without bitterness that
there's no way out. To have someone,

to never have to wake up alone with that still
small voice telling me I'm alive I'm
alive I'm alive.

Scarepigeon

Underneath the bridge I filled my coat
pockets with odd stones and shells unearthed
by high water. Upstream from the coal cranes,

in the shadow of sick trees, I found the pallet
shacks of the homeless and saw three men
sharing a pounder of Schlitz at the waterline,

griping at a passing limestone barge. The hazy
sun hung like a spider's egg in the trestle girders,
slipped beneath the clouds and cast

a giant shadow of myself against the brick
of a warehouse wall and for a moment
I was a monster on this earth.

I needn't have worried. The owl, carved lovingly
from a block of balsa, sat on its wonted
perch atop a tangle of feeder pipes

at the water treatment plant, skewered to a length of rebar
like the specimen of a long-vanished genus.
Pigeons perched beside her and whortled,

dusty from a daylong fast, desert fathers
come home to roost beside the mistress' throne.
I squatted and watched them and fingered the shells

in my pockets, city light pulsing like
mercury in the sky, the pig iron
clouds low above the bridges. And the moon,

a bootnail scuffed to base copper from that endless
backandforth across the factory floor.

Sunday Afternoons

The sunshine is plangent and numb like
violins sound. My hand slack on the drink like
it's crawled up on the glass and died there.
If there's such a thing

as judgment day my body will certainly testify against me.
Until then, there are books of greek heroes, a sandy
patch of ground beside the juniper behind the house,
cheap wine, even the talking of

lovely women, sometimes. Look, the housefinch has returned,
stropping her beak on the branch.
Birdhaunted as these afternoons are, of such inebriate
despair, of an exquisite hopelessness

like the day after the last day of the world, there remain
books of spanish history, of time's
unwanted children, of wanderings and home.
Odysseus in an open boat, the sun exhumed

and hung at dawn for another long day, so many lonely
nights from his beloved kingdom by the sea. O Poseidon,
make him suffer just a little longer.
Torquemada, I think he's ready.
Show him the instruments.

Meteor Shower

Men wearing canvas shoes and windbreakers
fill the Reading Room at the downtown library.
They sleep with glossy magazines spread on their knees

or read yesterday's paper with the front page photo
of a shirtless man on a grassy median, his taut neck filled
with what he's about to say, and three cops

poised, listening. All four look slightly ill.
Today's paper details the astronomer's forecast
accompanied by dark blue diagrams of the sky.

I pull one from a machine outside, walk to the bus stop shelter
and wait beside the retarded couple selling cigarette lighters and
pens on the sidewalk—crosslegged and dozing

before a carpet spread with gifts. Purple and white pigeons
lift from an air exchange grate. Raindrops
tick on the shelter's plastic roof. When night falls

I sit on the fire escape and watch the sky but it's been
washed clean by city lights and I can
only imagine stars falling, bright and angry and

everywhere at once. I picture a sky scored with fire,
foxes with torched tails panicking through the enemy's dark wheat.
After the world ends, we'll all meet again. We'll wake

with mild hangovers on a bright shore and watch
in silence as the white sails recede. We'll learn
all over again to make wine, wander

singly among the dunes, lost in our thoughts,
composing verses about stones and birds.
We'll be happy to the roots of our hearts,
and have no idea why we're crying.

Notes

"The Velvet Revolution, 1989–1990, v." *M1*, American main battle tank. *T-62*, Iraqi tank.

"The Groves of Ba'al." After *Lamentations*, iii, iv.

"Birds in March." *'the good spirits of the bells.'* From *The Waning of the Middle Ages*, by Johan Huizinga.

"Jupiter of the Wabash." *'doe-eyed bride of the monarch of the realms of the dead.'* From Bulfinch's *Mythology*.

"Elpenor." First line adapted from Pound's "Canto I."